The Inevitable

Dorothy Mahoney

The Inevitable

Text © 2022 Dorothy Mahoney

ISBN 978-1-958408-05-6

Red Moon Press
PO Box 2461
Winchester VA
22604-1661 USA
www.redmoonpress.com

Cover: Jean Bradley, *The Meeting*.
2010. Acrylic on canvas.
Used with permission.

first printing

for travel companions of the heart and page

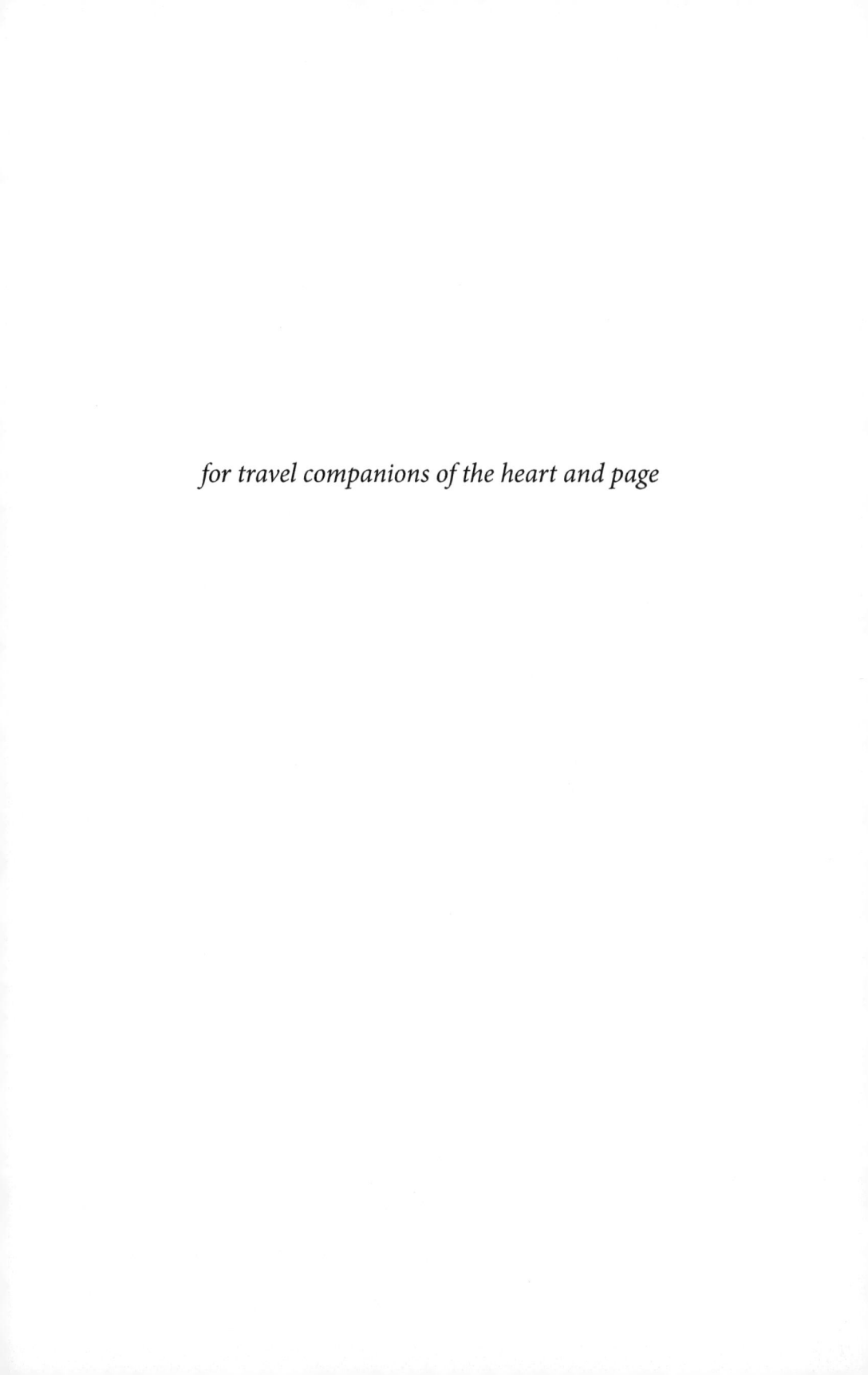

"Come closer! I will show you some magic. What is your name?"

Embroidery vendor near the Charles Bridge
Prague, 2019

The Inevitable

the inevitable

It is a trick. You know the kind. You choose three cards which return to the deck, cut the cards three times, and the dealer reveals which cards were chosen, one at a time as he reshuffles them. You are amazed each time and the dealer grins.

My plane ticket is cancelled three times: once for surgery, once to extend the time before and then to extend it after. There are three seats and each time an aisle is requested. After all of this, I switch seats so that three friends can sit together.

This is how I land in the seat next to the magician.

I do not reveal my name to strangers when I travel alone.

I immerse myself in a book. But the man leans in and talks as if he knows me, confides that he is going to visit his brother, to see his nephew. I listen. His props are in the overhead bin. Not the floating table though, not that. It is too big, awkward. He refuses to check the other items. They are expensive. He does parties. Pulls a deck of cards from his pocket and asks me if I want to see. The flight has just started and so I agree. He reaches over to release the food tray and starts to shuffle the cards.

He seems upset when I use the word 'magic.' He is not a 'magician'. He is an illusionist. He doesn't do 'magic' tricks. He practises illusions. I apologize.

I mention the 2006 film, "The Prestige" and my horror at the dead canary. Perhaps it should have been obvious when there were so many cages each containing a canary, that these were just inventory, that Michael Caine's character would pull another canary from his sleeve to suggest it was the original canary, flattened when the birdcage collapsed in order to 'disappear.' He shrugs and continues to shuffle the cards, asks if he should reveal the secret of The Inevitable. I say that won't be necessary.

I am curious what he considers to be the best illusion. His hands stop. There is a man in Boston who created a double deck of fifty cards. He would invite someone from the audience to mix them up on a board and he would marry the pairs. What kind of cards? Ordinary objects. Just ordinary objects. (Later I would search the Internet for more information, but never found anything to match his story.)

Who was this guy? A little too friendly, a little too knowing. The man next to him in the window seat has plugged his ears and fallen asleep. There is nothing I want him to know about me and so I pose questions he is happy to answer: where to buy props, how much they cost, when he first became interested in illusions and more of the same. I am half listening. What was the name of the notorious serial killer who dressed as a clown for birthday parties? I create an illusion of my own. Things are never what they seem. It is mid-flight and I am eager to see my friend waiting for me at the arrival gate. We are going to drive up the coast, drink wine and talk late nights. I hunger for her laughter, her Zen quality and calm. She can condense matter to its essence. She has that gift.

I ponder canaries. Then rabbits. What happens to them when they 'disappear' into black top hats?

The illusionist keeps talking.

The inevitable happens.

muse

Perhaps this is what inspired Dali. It was just like that. One day nothing. The next day, as if from nowhere, ants crawling over and under everything: the dirty dishes left on the counter the night before . . . running madly over the knives and forks, rimming the morning coffee cups, darting in the bread drawer, the recycling bin, the dog's food dish. There are no melting clocks, but the ants rally quickly over the spot of strawberry jam dripped accidently on the headline of the morning paper. The dog seems nonplussed; she prefers moths.

>outside, in
>the fruit dish is a face
>on the beach

amateur

He seems to know what he is doing. Who called him? Here he is, confident in his beekeeping mask, wearing sandals, scooping up the bees into a cardboard box. They had been twirling and landing on the cement planter, until the bees formed a dark, twitching mass that had attracted the attention of many crossing the sidewalk, on their way to work downtown that morning. The bees are quiet. Cars rush back and forth between traffic lights. A horn blares. Somewhere a jackhammer breaks up cement. The man gently continues to fill the box, scooping bees with his fingers.

> beehive
> so many bobby pins
> in place

from the depths

Just numbers: 10 tons and 14 metres long. A sperm whale on a beach in Uruguay; crane and bulldozer in primary colours, like children's toys, maneuvering. Someone with outstretched arms is trying to size the tail. It has been dead for days, drifting in like a page from a storybook, the wooden boy and his father swallowed by Monstro, looking up at the cathedral of ribs.

> goliath heart
> heavier than I
> can bear

on the road

He never would have wanted this, his daughter vows. After her father's death, so much about the funeral is a guess. He wants to be cremated, but what about a service, music, an urn. He was a hardworking man, so his ashes are poured into his steel thermos and sit temporarily on the bookshelf. After the burglary, it isn't the first thing missed since the teens make a mess in the bathrooms, look for pharmaceuticals and steal all the liquor bottles from the den. They confess to emptying the thermos from the car window when it isn't cocaine.

>missing the exit
>unable to turn back
>plowed fields

memory keeper

This is not my story. I tell it, as if it is, so that you believe. You will not think that this is possible. That this could happen here. That one can survive.

I know.

Soon these will be the words of no one. I hear this from one who survived but is no more. Someone eating cherries, someone like you.

Even now, this tree grown from ash, this street, where the old street buckled. These houses, where other houses crumbled. A flash of light and then, black rain. Shadows cast on walls; everyone turns to ghosts.

> paint thin twigs dark
> thicker ones light
> leave empty space for cherry blossom

somewhere else

Rain is what they pray for. Elsewhere rain is a curse turning roads into rivers, forcing people onto rooftops, here roads course with cars, their rear-view mirrors black with ash and soot, buildings and rooftops collapse into billowing smoke. Somewhere ahead hovers hope: survivors, safety, someplace to stop, to summon others, to sleep. If only the skies would open and flood this hell, force the flames to flare, sizzle, smoulder. If only there was enough time to turn back and take more of what is left behind. Somewhere else prayers rise for heat.

    burn mapping
    fire spreads
    over paper

Snake River

When she sees her son cut and bleeding, she thinks the worst has happened. But he has escaped death, run home in the darkness. She wants to save him, washes the blood away, wraps him with torn sheets, tries to calm him. He is back on the bed of his childhood. Let this not be his shroud, she thinks. Let this not be. But too soon they do come. She would give anything. Take the two cows for my son. Anything. She begs. Begs. They say they will take him to hospital, but she knows well where he is going.

>full moon
>the river
>writhing

"Do you hear that?" he whispers, "They are starting to pray!"

Despite the lurching waves, a man's shape stands in the gloom with his hands high.

A few of the migrants in the crowded boat chant with him.

"Mercy! Protect us! Hear us! Fill our hearts with peace, help bring this boat ashore . . ."

With each repeated phrase, the sea rises and strikes their frightened faces. Someone is crying.

"It's only getting worse. His prayers are angering the waters. We will all perish in this storm!" He grabs a board at his feet. "Help me save us."

>deck of cards
>turn the top one
>over

disappeared

You can follow the vultures, circling, and you can walk the roadside ditches, search where the weeds are thickest. Sometimes, someone will whisper, there are places in the hills where rocks are rearranged.

You can lean a shovel against the house, ready.

Sometimes you can imagine waking up and he's back. His shoes have moved, his chair is pulled back, his bed unmade. But you are only waking up. You want to sense his presence. It has been too long for worry now. If they march to your door, you will act sincere, say he is gone to the city.

> on the back stoop
> a pair of work boots
> missing tongues

nail house

There is a house in the middle of the highway. The electricity and the water have been cut off. Traffic rushes around it as if it was a mountain too obstinate to dynamite and tunnel through. The authorities have been unable to persuade, threaten or entice relocation. The occupants are elderly and will eventually die. This is not the only house, not the only owners willing to take a stand in a country where rebellion is dangerous, where compliance is the norm. Eventually the house will also die, nothing left, the hammer will pound flat the stubborn nail.

    resurfacing
    red tulips
    in the bulldozed lot

persuasion

He has become his father, he thinks, as he carries water to his ancient home. He is stooped and his pace slow. He knows there are those who wish him gone, say he should take the money and move into a modern building. They say he cannot survive here without power. His father spoke often of his childhood, carting water from the river, living by the light of the sun, the moon, eating what was fresh, knowing how to get by. But this is not easy. A stranger waits for him at his door. The water spills from the pail.

    moonlight
    convinces
    the blind mirror

sacred destination

They are both on a high-speed bullet train, the old man who is a travelling singer of ancient ballads and the younger woman who is thankful for a safe and peaceful life. She intends to offer prayers at the Shinto Shrine. He intends to set himself on fire. He offers the other passengers around him paper notes, tells them to please move back, that it is dangerous. He is dangerous.

He dumps the fuel from the plastic container over his head, over some of the seats. She is unaware that this is happening. The train blurs the landscape speeding ahead.

> waiting for the train
> to pass
> cat on a hunt

that Friday

It is only a number, but the morning begins with a headache that will not quiet with coffee, that persists beyond the crease of noon. "Take something," he says, "or go sleep it off." It is a Friday devoid of witches' cats and ladders, no murderer with a chainsaw masked in the closet, no storms, just a headache, like a watchmaker tapping and turning, tinkering with the mechanism. Perhaps that is how it begins. Bad luck.

Two tablets in the palm and water, asleep all afternoon, waking unaware of day. The watch face crowded with a new number between twelve and one.

>   tiger launching
>   from another tiger's mouth
>   bee and pomegranate

signature

They grow not far from the kitchen. Silver-gray, cardoons, a favourite vegetable on the menu.

The stalks pared of thistles and blanched, served in spirals with black truffles. Some save for a year to dine here. All is seasonal, the crockery sold and replaced five times annually, a new menu created each time. It is about change as in nature. He likes to walk his dog in the woods; he likes cooking with mushrooms. They define the seasons. He is found by a friend having used his own hunting rifle. No one can understand why.

>final accounting
>no note
>in his hand

empty cup

There is nothing to talk about. Many are silent. Shake their heads. This is a country that scores high on the happiness index, a country of few psychiatrists, where suicide hotlines shut down from underuse, where counselors become matchmakers instead. What to believe in an atheist state. The old believe they have three sons: the Medicine Son, the Rope Son and the Water Son, death by pesticide, hanging or drowning. These are the reliable sons. There are no others here, gone to the city, or gone. What to do when you turn grey, alone and unable 'to taste the tea.'

    3 upside down cups
    a stone
    under 1

miracle

This is what they say. This is the handshake of hope. When the world you know collapses around you, on top of you, pins you down, lets you speak when others cease. Call their names, but they cannot answer. Then, in the darkness, there is nothing else. In the dust of brick and mortar, in promises that staircase from this collapse, there is this landing. Strangers lift their sorrow, wipe tears and applaud that you are found that you are real. But you know, you are not you. With one leg gone, there will be no work in the fields, no work in the new brickyard.

>   hearing his voice
>   but not
>   the words he says

peak

He says his parents are resting down by the river. He is waiting for relatives. They will come for the funeral when they can. There is much rubble to search. Mountains.

He says he saw them last on Mother's Day, a cheerful family meal. His mother's famous dumplings, his father's homemade beer. He knows it was quick. His mother electrocuted on the roof top by falling wires, his father hit by a beam on the staircase. Perhaps she had sent him back for her shawl. Perhaps it was a voice calling from the door below.

>house of cards
>a steady breath
>in both hands

over

There are stories that are repeated, but many were given up, like closed suitcases left at the curb for garbage collection. They become refuse. It is like that, starting over. The hope that suitcases are no longer needed. That this is a fresh start, with new language, new faces, newness like a thin coat not warm enough in colder climate. Perhaps there are a few names like old handshakes. Old words that keep hearts warm like a hot water bottle in a bed, beginning to cool until it is touched. It is like that.

> name change
> dropping the ending
> for a new start

teeth

She pulls the steel comb down through her long hair and acknowledges herself in the mirror.

She does not look as old as the women back home. She still feels young. She pulls on her boots and slips her arms into the sleeves of her coat, wraps a long shawl around her neck and goes to the subway station. Everyone is going somewhere, rushing. She reaches for the escalator railing and glides forward, feels a tug. A sharp tug. Her shawl. She lurches to free it. Staggers. Her hair grabs forward over her face, catches and wrenches her down.

    silk scarf
    all the knots
    open wide

crossing with the light

We are waiting at the corner, ready to go one way, but go the other as that light changes.

It is a wide intersection and strangers are with us, against us, in a rush to get to either side as numbers flash in the countdown.

"Remember the last time you were here?"

I watch my feet, stepping carefully over the grooves and the shiny rails of the streetcar.

"Not really," I answer honestly, head down.

"Yes. Some woman was hit by the streetcar. Killed. Her bag of groceries spilled."

Before she says more, I conjure oranges, rolling, rolling.

>juggling
>all the planets
>revolving at once

flames and fireworks

Shops are closed and people gather in the square. A vodka bottle is passed hand to hand and a tray of sandwiches. Others sing passionately or shout slogans. There are flags and banners, fireworks and barricades of tires and wooden desks, chairs, create a swelling smoke that obscures the view of the opposite side. Someone is smashing the sidewalk with a sledgehammer and there is a heavy tremor of approaching tanks. There are bats and balaclavas, rocks and rubber bullets. Someone says there are at least twenty-five dead, but who can tell in the darkness.

>after the news footage
>cereal commercial
>and the weather

never been

It's a lie. I have touched down in Paris several times. Brief layovers on the way to somewhere else.

Always aghast at the price of processed cheese between slices of white bread. Stale. Recognizing the not-French by their sloppy logo clothing, slumping in wait mode for the next flight announcement.

Wanting to be on a bicycle near the Eiffel tower with a fresh baguette. Wanting to think French.

"Ever been to Paris?"

I say, "No."

> how Copperfield
> makes the Eiffel Tower
> reappear

key

Someone is playing a piano inside a brick building It may be Bach or Brahms, but that does not matter.

The music is outside now: brightens petunias in the flowerboxes, the short sharp steps of a terrier on a leash, and the buttons on his owner's jacket. It squeezes between the movement of cars and buses and opens the new leaves in the trees. It stops the man reading the newspaper, presses aside suffering, war and genocide, even a sparrow pauses. The pianist practices every morning like this; the oldest survivor of the camps, plays from memory.

somewhere close by lilacs

the same scene

It is a quiet house. There is one vehicle in the driveway and a basketball net. Surprised neighbors converge across the street, repeat lines scripted from other scenes. This is a quiet neighborhood. I didn't know them, but they never caused any trouble. They seemed like good people. This is something that you see on TV. How could this happen in our neighborhood. Why here?

Police tape stretches around the base of a lamp post to a fence separating the house from the next property. A second-floor window gapes.

>   subdivision
>   shadeless streets
>   named after trees

blunt force

He knew how to cook chicken feet, the oil spat from the skillet, the sizzle as he turned them. Once wings were this cheap until every bar served them, jacked the price. Feet are a best-kept secret. Outside the cicadas are shrill, and he is so hungry, tired. Now, the new hire who had been sleeping in cars, slipping into shelters, now, this know-it-all sleeps here. He says feet need more spice as he snatches one from the pan.

"Hey! You owe me at least a cigarette, man!"

His leer answers back until the cutting board comes down on his head.

> grease trap
> cockroaches between
> stacked plates

firing range

"You know, it's very relaxing shooting a gun," he confides. "Think about it. If you ever want to come along, give me a call."

I lean back in my chair. Thank him for the offer. "I've gone skeet shooting years ago. I don't think I could ever kill anything."

"It's target practice. That's all." He remembers something. "You know the family tree information you asked about? Well, I gave it to a distant relative. I'll have to ask his mother for it. Poor guy got esophageal cancer and shot himself in the bathroom. Gives guns a bad name."

> safety catch
> no ammo
> in the chamber

crossing

And then there was nothing else to say anymore. The silence widened like a river fed by spring runoff, cold and bitter.

Woods grew on either side. One thick and impenetrable, with conifers and conspirators, lies and threats; the other, sparse with saplings, scattered birds migrating, a marsh of hopelessness, the smell of something in ashes.

The travelled routes begin to disappear and there are no maps for this new country.

She forms an apology and tries to reach him, but it falls and sinks like a rock in the middle of the river, where it splashes against him.

>spring melt
>all the names
>he gave her

eggs over hard

He licks the knife. Having breakfast with his old neighbor is a welcome surprise. He signals the waitress over for a refill of coffee. Sticks out his mug. There are so many questions he wants to ask about his ex-wife but realizes he must appear nonchalant. He has been watching. He knows her boyfriend. Follows him. Knocks over his garbage cans, punctures his tire, steals his mail. Calls the Children's Aid and makes a false report. Now his daughters no longer see him. He once taught them to sing, "Your Cheatin' Heart."

    egged on
    empty carton
    on the curb

frozen

Let's pretend. He holds their small hands. Let's make believe this is a castle. We are not who we are. Outside the real snow has covered the real hotel, has covered the real roads, cars, covered where we come from. Here we are. Let's pretend you are the princess. You be the reindeer and you be the snowman. Let's pretend your favourite movie.

    "Let it go"
    repeating the chorus
    loud, louder

leaper

His mother always said he was unreliable. Laughs. It is a family joke and some years when he was young he worried there would be no birthday for him. No cake, no presents, nothing. This is how his older brothers tease. "Do you see a date here?" They point to the end of February with its white space, the number 28 like the last step on a pool ladder plunging into nothingness. The Titanic sank on a leap year they chant. This goes on for years until his mother amends the calendar with a magic marker.

>jumping over
>the 9 on one foot
>hopscotch

city landscape

The scream sounded human and rose in decibels into the leafing trees on the boulevard, across the

mowed lawns and the flower beds of marigolds and pink petunias. There were only so many places to hide: under cars, behind hedges or beneath decks with lattice chewn or shifted. The sound could not be ignored although the windows and doors of the houses were locked. Sparrows dispersed from feeders and a robin left the birdbath, disturbed. A dog started barking. Earlier a piece of plywood had been nailed over a broken attic vent, the mother raccoon despondent.

    knocking
    the robin nest
    down again

gift

There is no safe, she realizes after praying for months that her unborn child will be. There is no answer. Even the Pope saying that birth control is permissible. Nothing is the way it was, no matter how often she bows her head in prayer, no matter what she promises. She wants to believe in miracles but when the baby arrives, his head is too small, his arms twisted. She gives him a name, kisses him, his dark eyes distant. She leaves his body behind, to save others.

>pigeons mass
>monument to those saved
>from plague

offering

She brings her black cake, rum-soaked, to the missionary's house. She has promised, after his jokes about Christmas fruitcake and doorstops. She thinks tarts with sorrel jam and sweet potato pudding. Imagines snow like sifted flour or peaks of beaten egg whites But none of that, she knocks to find the door open, all insides upside down, blood, and he is missing. She forgets the cake at the door.

>roadside shrine
>how constant
>the weeds

coconut

I do not know 'albinism', I think 'coconut', my brown belly so round, my baby inside, so white. Little ghost. So valuable. My husband thinks money to change our lives: so much for her fingers, her arms, her heart. Poison her, my neighbor says, so much better now then to have her disappear. To know she is a lucky charm, that fishermen would weave her hair into their nets, miners wear her tiny bones from strings around their necks. My little ghost. I wish her brown, safe as a coconut high in a tree.

      sun-tipped fronds
      weaver's nest sways
      out of reach

payment

The money is tucked in a secret pocket she sews into her waistband.

She pretends it isn't there, especially when she hears that Shreya is dead.

Her hands guided her difficult babies into this world. She is the one to convince her to be done with birth. They will both be paid and never worry again. Shreya agrees.

Now it is done. She is not responsible for the incompetence of doctors. No.

She saves Shreya with every birth. She would die having another. It was never about the money. No. Never.

> wrist of bangles
> alms chime
> in the beggar's cup

harvest

The truck is empty when the girls climb in. The metal floor echoes as they jump up and down in their sneakers, giggling at the first bolt forward when the wheels begin to turn. The hopper showers canola seeds and wisps of stalk and dry leaf. They back away from the spray, still giggling, stoop to fill their hands as it fills the space around their feet, climbs up their ankles, holds their knees. They slow as if in water. But there is dust. There is a deep rumble. They reach to each other, towards the metal ladder. To the air above.

>so yellow
>tourists snap photos
>bright fields against blue skies

switch

She looks like her mother, now. Even the mothers were not sure when their babies return from a treatment for jaundice. Their hair length was different, or so they thought, but then again, no. Then years later, in anger, one father slugs his wife with an insult that the girl looks like no one, that his wife must have slept around. The test proves she is not theirs. But by then, she is. Too late at ten to switch the girls, too late to wrong the right. The girl with the long hair shrugs exactly like her other mother.

>cowbird
>counterfeit egg
>with the warblers

contents

What is in the freezer: a package of weightless hot dog buns, dried out fish sticks, a suitcase. What's in the suitcase? A could-be answer for a custom's officer, a pair of shoes, socks, missing underwear, a wrinkled dress, a hairbrush. An answer for a curious child on the subway; be glad it's not you. An answer for a stranger waiting for the next stop: a question at our feet, which squeezes us tight and even tighter. A suitcase can be dropped into a river or a garbage bin, burned in a vacant lot, stored in a freezer.

>luggage tag
>none of the blanks
>filled in

survivors

They sit together and listen. The speaker confesses that she does not have the disease but that she works with many who do and she feels she has an understanding. She asks if they oppose the term and adds that if she could, she would call them "thrivers." She wants to empower them. Give them back some control. She talks about the physical and emotional signs of depression and fatigue. Says there comes a time to find new meaning in life. Be open to change. Talk about issues. When the session ends, they walk back into the dark night.

    fireflies
    extinguished
    by morning

tomorrow

He prays, his knees trembling with the vibrations of the dirt floor, closes his stinging eyes. Feels the air thicken, the heat comes now and soon the ash. Breathing and wondering how his prayers had appeased before, and the offerings, how yesterday he said he did not know about tomorrow, only today. How his brother recites a dream of his father, of him, and how serene he can make himself feel, stooping low, knowing the roof will collapse. That he is the one appointed to make the volcano calm, the spiritual gatekeeper, that with supplication, his submission is enough.

>   prayer
>   the sweep of light
>   through darkness

fateful day

This is a day of fanfare and finery. Months of anticipation and careful planning from mountains of marigolds to one hundred dishes of curries and tandoori. Even the horses' hooves are diligently polished, their manes combed and braided with ribbons. It is rumored the streets between the groom's house and the future bride were broomed by relatives the night before. Now the procession begins with music and jubilation. Guns fire. The street is a blur of colour and commotion. Birds fly from the trees skyward. The groom slumps over his horse, falls, and everyone rushes forward.

    all eyes
    peacock's tail
    hue and cry

somebody, somebody

According to police, somebody tips the contents of the suitcase discovered on the side of the highway. Perhaps a victim of too many gangster movies, the getaway car jettisons cash during a pursuit. So, seeking treasure, the finder grips the zipper of the faded canvas and tugs it open, full of hope, but a Pandora's box of misery is exposed. One pink shoe, a black tutu, the small pink pants spill and the suitcase drops. Somebody runs. Others report a man carrying a similar case weeks earlier. Somebody must have noticed her missing. Perhaps missing years ago. Somebody must be missing her somewhere.

> playground
> all the children gone
> cigarette butts

repair

In the dark, a drunken man slips into a crater by the road. Accidentally, the repair crew fill it with gravel and asphalt, then smooth it over with a roller. Police dig up the road when someone reports seeing the hand. The road is paved again. The funeral procession must travel this way and the man's friends and family must travel back this same way. The asphalt smell is strong in the afternoon sun, the edges soft.

>   detour
>   blue flag wave
>   from the ditch

unhappen

It's like knitting, she thinks. That unraveling that allows her to start over with the same yarn, pulling, stretching, and wrapping it by hand into a tighter ball called different day. Delay waking a little longer, stir the porridge more slowly, go up the stairs to kiss them rather than calling them down to the breakfast table. Or have it rain, a storm to flood the fields, or have the cow begin to calf early. Or the boys wake with fevers and they stay home. Anything that keeps the tractor in the barn, the steep ditch empty of their crushed forms.

    magic trick
    the same day
    somewhere else

tea box

It is sad, she agrees, but going to estate sales makes you appreciate other lives, the collecting and collecting, the joy of all that, then the dispersal, finding the treasure in the treasure of others. Seeing the value in what others dismiss as debris of the deceased. A recent acquisition is her tea box. It is the size of an ottoman, the inside lined with tin, the outside covered in a faded pattern. The agent insists, all contents included, layers of scrap fabric. Emptying it on her kitchen floor, she unfolds a wedding kimono.

> gunpowder tea
> the dregs portend
> a journey

near

I left no lights on and now there is no beacon. There is no one at the window, and no one at the door, no one under my blanket to keep my bed warm. I know I am close, jingle the pocket with keys, my fingers numb. In this tunnel of snow, I could be anywhere, only my thoughts to compass me home. There is no sidewalk, no road, and all the trees have vanished into cutting coldness. There is no fence to follow, no hand reaching for mine. I don't know where I am. I might be close.

> white out
> squinting to find
> what is erased

water

Some perch on the roof while others sit or stand inside with chickens and goats. The bus has four wheels on the road and then does not. It was a rock hurling down the embankment, a rock sinking into a deep rush and swirl of more rocks and confusion that is the river. The ripples begin with the few thrown from the roof, caught like debris in the trees, and witnesses who hear the crushing metal, much farther. Others wait impatiently to board the bus that will not arrive.

>   bus driver's wife
>   plops potatoes
>   into the soup

at the door

He becomes a believer when he opens the door. It has been a quiet new year. He is reciting the Frost poem about woods dark and deep and promises. The yard light is on, illuminating the drive and the front stairs. His dachshunds start barking. There is a raccoon that likes to raid the suet feeder. A faint knock. His neighbors are summer occupants only. He shushes the dogs. It is a girl wearing shorts and a light top. She has no shoes, just one sock. Her nose is bleeding. There was a plane crash. She follows his light.

    snow angel
    pushing off
    from the wings

gone

The night we will best see Saturn, the moon does not appear, and we crane our necks to scan the whole sky, but nothing shines. So often we look up but see nothing. In that sky, linked to all our skies, so many things missed, a plane traveling in the night never reaching its destination, passengers still up there, eyes closed, sleeping in our minds.

>luna moth
>attracted by the yard light
>wings wide

string

Floating on a breeze. The same sky, same clouds, same sun to squint at and desire for some height, some command, some recognition. Some fly without wind, know how to manoeuvre a kite over and around rooftops, satellite dishes, familiar trees. So much to know, so much for advantage, shape, size, material and then the string. Invisible, coated with glass shards, to take down the kites of rivals. The same sky, same clouds, the celebration. Neighbors and friends look up, look and all their necks stretched so, and the glass-coated string, invisible cuts through the air.

>   out of the blue
>   knot
>   in the kite spool

The plane lands and it is time to disembark. With no checked luggage I head to the exit.

Inside the terminal, my friend waves. I look back momentarily but the illusionist is no longer there. I reach into my pocket and find my folded boarding pass and three cards.

acknowledgments

The prose pieces began as daily 100 word flash fictions inspired by news events and created on Drablr.

Thank you to the Drablr writing community for comments and support.

Thank you to Madeline Sonik who was the University of Windsor's writer in residence at the time, read some of the drabbles and suggested an experimental novel.

Thank you to Arleen Pare for suggesting the title early on, over dinner.

Thank you to Terry Ann Carter for showing the way and waiting at the airport.

An earlier version of 'amateur' appeared as 'bees' in *By the River* (Urban Farmhouse Press, 2017).

The haiku that begins ' prayer' won honorable mention in the Romanian International Haiku Contest in 2020.

'From the depths' was published in *Contemporary Haibun Online* (CHO) fall 2021.

'Tea Box" was published in *after the fall*, The Trillium Haiku Group Anthology 2021.

With gratitude to Jim Kacian and "the river / the river makes / of the moon".

Dorothy Mahoney is the author of several poetry books, including *Off-Leash* (2016) and *Ceaseless Rain* (2020, both Palimpsest Press). *The Inevitable* began as *drabble* exercises in response to newspaper articles. After completing a Buson challenge, writing ten haiku a day for 100 days, the matching haiku evolved. Her work has appeared in various anthologies including: *Erotic haiku: of Skin on Skin* (Black Moss Press, 2017), *Jar of Rain* (Red Moon Press, 2020) and *The Wanderer Brush, The Art of Haiga,* edited and illustrated by Ion Codrescu (Red Moon Press, 2020). A haibun based on her volunteer work at Hospice was recognized in the Genjuan International Haibun Contest in Japan. She is a retired teacher who spends much time with family at the cottage on Manitoulin Island with Oliver, an Old English sheepdog.